Baby and Beyond

Progression in Play for Babies and Children

Tell Me a Story

This edition published 2013
First published 2009 by Featherstone, an imprint of
Bloomsbury Publishing plc
50 Bedford Square, London,
www.bloomsbury.com

ISBN 978-1-4081-9499-7

Text © Clare Beswick 2009
Illustrations © Martha Hardy
Series editor, Sally Featherstone
Cover image © Shutterstock
Photo (p.6) © LEYF/Emli Bendixen

First published in the UK, 2009 by Featherstone Education Ltd

Printed and bound in India by Replika Press Pvt Ltd

This book is produced using paper that is made from wood grown in managed, sustainable forests. It is natural, renewable and
recyclable. The logging and manufacturing processes conform to the environmental regulations of the country of origin.

To see our full range of titles
visit **www.bloomsbury.com**

Contents

Baby and Beyond

A series of books for practitioners working with children from birth to five and beyond

This book gives ideas for introducing and extending storytelling activities and experiences for babies and young children. Each page spread contains a range of experiences and a selection of ideas for each of the six stages in Development Matters (Revised EYFS 2012). Developmental stages 4, 5 and 6 have been combined over two sections:

Birth–11 months	8–20 months	16–26 months	22–36 months	36–60+ months
Developmental Stage 1	Developmental Stage 2	Developmental Stage 3	Developmental Stages 4 and 5	Developmental Stages 5 and 6

For babies and young children the advantages of listening to stories told from memory or read aloud from a picture book are well researched. Sharing stories is great fun and creates a special bond between the teller and the listener, developing a sense of shared sustained attention and interaction. Reading aloud to babies and children enhances their skills across all areas of learning and development. The sharing of stories is a fundamental part of the EYFS, particularly in the areas of development of Communication and Language and Literacy.

Listening to stories provides children with new friends, and characters they can try out in new situations such as role play and their own storytelling. Sharing and telling stories enables them to make connections with others' experiences and emotions. The act of listening extends children's ability to maintain their attention and develop important skills, such as turn taking, associated with being part of a group.

The wealth of language and variety of styles and rhythms that can be presented through storytelling enhances communication skills. It provides children with a rich language and a plethora of ideas to draw on as they become storytellers and later writers themselves. Enjoying poetry, rhymes, rhyming text and nonsense tales sparks in children a love of words and develops their sense of fun and creativity.

Storytelling is a fundamental element in all cultures, and traditional tales are a great way for children to get to know their own and other cultures and times. But most of all, sharing stories is great fun and creates a sense of well being and joy, for everyone from tiny babies onwards.

Tell Me a Story is laid out in progression across the EYFS, showing how storytelling can be used and developed for tiny babies, and developed to meet the interests and needs of older children towards the end of the EYFS. Much emphasis is placed on encouraging interaction and spontaneity. This book aims to give early years practitioners the confidence, skills and knowledge of how to use a wide variety of books and storytelling techniques across the whole of the EYFS, from traditional tales to books without words, digital storytelling and nonsense rhymes. We would encourage practitioners to delve into the incredible wealth and breadth of books available as well as drawing on their own and the children's resources, and the traditional tales of familiar and less familiar cultures, to provide an environment rich and varied in storytelling and sharing books.

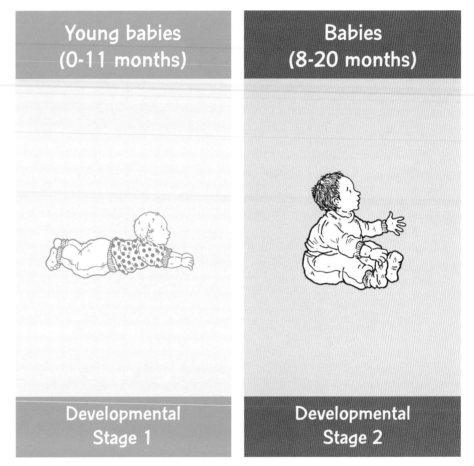

Young babies (0-11 months)	Babies (8-20 months)
Developmental Stage 1	Developmental Stage 2

Young children (16-26 months)	Children (22-36 months)	Older children (36-60+ months)

Developmental Stage 3	Developmental Stages 4 & 5	Developmental Stages 5 & 6

Traditional stories

Traditional stories told from memory, or from favourite books at home and in early years settings, give babies and young children a sense of warmth and belonging. With repetition of key phrases, common themes and thought-provoking messages, traditional stories can be used right across the EYFS.

Young babies (0-11 months)

Very young babies love the warmth and attention of familiar words, songs and rhymes. Choose just two or three favourite traditional finger play rhymes and build these into your everyday times together, or with your key babies. Try 'tickle' rhymes, 'peek-a-boo' songs and 'jogging on the knee' rhymes. All these are great foundations for later traditional story rhymes, songs and books.

Developmental Stage 1

Babies (8-20 months)

Older babies will love turning the pages of favourite titles, and pointing to familiar pictures in simple board books relating to traditional stories. Focus on the key repeated phrases such as 'Huff and puff and blow your house down' in the *Three Little Pigs* story. Link actions to these phrases, such as a gentle blow on the babies fingers with 'huff and puff'. Many babies will begin to 'tell' themselves the story in sounds as they turn the pages.

Developmental Stage 2

Young children (16-26 months)

Goldilocks and the Three Bears is a perfect introduction to traditional stories for this age. With lots of repetition of key phrases, and the emphasis on first words, such as cup, spoon, bowl, chair and house, a simple short version of this story told or sung will capture the attention of children at this developmental stage. Keep things simple by using just a few everyday objects as props, such as three wooden spoons, three plastic bowls or three teddy bears.

Children (22-36 months)

At this stage you can involve the children by pausing in the telling of familiar traditional tales so children can add their own words. With older children, stop and ask them what happens next. Link the traditional story told from memory or following a picture book to other activities, such as simple role play or creative activities. These provide excellent opportunities to reinforce the simple language and joy of sharing familiar stories.

Older children (36-60+ months)

Introduce older children to a wealth of traditional stories. Look for different books retelling the same story. Invite the children to join in the telling of the story. Encourage parents and grandparents to come into the setting to share traditional tales from their own childhood. Extend this with some simple Google searching for traditional tales on line. And of course, don't miss '*Each Peach Pear Plum*' by Janet and Allan Ahlberg – a book about stories.

Picture books

There is a myriad of amazing, beautifully illustrated picture books we can share with babies and young children. Choose carefully as they will form the foundations for babies' and young children's joy of books as well as becoming central to the development of their creativity and thinking skills.

Young babies (0-11 months)

Reading aloud builds bonds between babies and early years practitioners, especially their 'key people' in the setting and at home. Look out for simple board books that are visually interesting and focus the baby's attention on the page. Share black and white pattern books, as well as books with a range of textures, colours and patterns to explore. Look for books with ribbons to pull, buzzers to find, as well as holes to poke tiny fingers through.

Developmental Stage 1

Babies (8-20 months)

At this stage, babies are fascinated by pictures of other babies. Look for photo books and stories with clear bright illustrations. Give babies lots of opportunity to look at the pictures. From time to time point out familiar objects and ask babies to find familiar objects. Provide simple books with rhyming or repeating text around themes familiar to the child. Favourite themes at this stage will include home, babies, cars and buses.

Developmental Stage 2

Young children (16-26 months)

Look for picture books with great beginnings that grab attention, text with a simple clear story, and a satisfying and safe ending. Illustrations are hugely important at this stage. Choose books with a wide variety of styles of illustrations. Young children love stories that involve collecting objects or searching for something. Encourage the children to join in with repeated phrases and to imitate simple actions that you link to key words in the picture book.

Children (22-36 months)

Now children will be enjoying a wealth of different styles of picture books. Share the books with individuals or very small groups of children, allowing plenty of time to look at each page. Reinforce the theme of the picture book by finishing with a rhyme, song or object of the same theme. Extend the learning through role play, such as providing a washing line, clothes and pegs after reading 'Mrs Mopple's Washing Line' or 'Walter's Windy Washing day'.

Older children (36-60+ months)

By this stage children should enjoy listening to more complex picture book stories and retelling the story with and without the book.

Introduce a range of picture books on a wide variety of themes from different cultures.

Encourage children to discuss the stories and to talk about why they like particular books. Talk about the characters and their different situations. All this will allow children to make connections with others' personal experiences.

Developmental Stage 3

Developmental Stages 4 & 5

Developmental Stages 5 & 6

Books without words

Books without words offer an exceptional opportunity. Sharing these books is open ended, and allows practitioners and children to use their imagination and creativity freely. It also enables the practitioner to fine tune how they will vary the story as they retell it for individual babies or children.

Young babies (0-11 months)

Look for simple board books with photographs of babies doing lots of different familiar things. Babies love to look at other babies and such books will ensure lots of smiles and opportunities for interaction. Also provide books with different textures, shapes and mirrors to explore.

Developmental Stage 1

Babies (8-20 months)

Older babies can search for familiar objects in photograph books. Find books that you can sing along to, providing a simple commentary on the illustrations, or perhaps making animal and other sounds for babies to imitate. By this stage, babies will enjoy pointing to show you items on request as well as pointing to draw your attention to things they find interesting. Encourage imitation of sounds as well as actions to reinforce the story.

Developmental Stage 2

Young children (16-26 months)

Simple story books without words such as 'Rosie's Walk', 'Sunshine' 'Moonlight' or 'The Little Mouse' enable you to share the same book with children at different developmental stages, maybe first imitating the sounds and actions, following the animals with a finger and so on. Pause in the telling of the story for children to join in with or fill in familiar words and key phrases, and to think about what might happen next.

Children (22-36 months)

At this stage pause more often to let children predict what might happen on the next page. Try and create links between what you see on the pages and the children's own worlds. Ask open ended questions to encourage the children to talk about their own culture and experiences. Look out for books without words that offer children an opportunity to talk about and think about how the characters feel – try 'The Snowman' by Raymond Briggs.

Older children (36-60+ months)

Use props and familiar everyday objects or small world toys to encourage children to retell the story in their own words and following the pictures in books without words.

Encourage children to take turns with each page of story-telling and to help each other out. At this stage children love stories about searching and chases, and stories about animals. Try working together with individuals or small groups to create your own 'books without words' using photos.

Developmental Stage 3

Developmental Stages 4 & 5

Developmental Stages 5 & 6

Poetry and rhyme

From first finger rhymes and tickle play to long poems with a story and poetry from around the world, poetry and rhyme offer special opportunities to play with words. They also help children to grasp the sheer joy of songs and rhymes, as well as firing their enjoyment, energy and creativity.

Young babies (0-11 months)

Tiny babies will enjoy gentle tickle rhymes and finger play. As the months go by, encourage babies to imitate simple actions, try 'just like me' first, turn taking in actions and rewarding vocalisations with smiles, tickles and more fun. Clapping rhymes help children with imitating and with feeling a sense of rhythm. Try dancing with babies, singing the rhymes as you sway and turn, dip and twirl.

Developmental Stage 1

Babies (8-20 months)

Take time to find a wide variety of simple rhymes in anthologies or collections. These are widely available in print, on line and as audio tapes and DVDs. Try rhymes that combine words with simple actions. Strong repeated key phrases will grab the attention of babies at this stage of development. Use just one simple prop, preferably an everyday object that links with the rhyme to focus babies' attention and build on the activity.

Developmental Stage 2

Young children (16-26 months)

Look for rhymes and poetry that combine active play with great text, such as 'Doing the Animal Bop' by Jan Ormerod and Lindsay Gardiner. Few young children will be able to resist joining in with this sort of rhyme, and the pictures offer a great focus for looking at the rhyme time and time again. Search for rhyming picture books such as 'Brown Bear, Brown Bear, What do you See?' by Eric Carle, by using a search engine such as Google.

Children (22-36 months)

Think about the text and words used in favourite first poems and rhymes. Look for poems with different beats, and rich and varied language, accessible to very young children. Try using multi-sensory props, such as something to taste, smell or feel that links with the poem. Poems and rhymes with actions are great for children at this stage. Encourage children to imitate actions and make up their own to go with key phrases or words in poems.

Older children (36-60+ months)

Create treasure baskets of objects linked to poems and rhymes. At this stage, role play is central to a child's world, so be sure to offer suitable dressing up clothes and props, real and symbolic, to enable children to play out their favourite poems and rhymes. This is a good stage to introduce poems and rhymes from around the world as well as those from the culture of children living in your local community. Ask parents to help you make a collection of these.

Developmental Stage 3

Developmental Stages 4 & 5

Developmental Stages 5 & 6

Create your own stories

Stories tailored to a child or small group of children, or listening and creating stories together, are very important. They enable practitioners to adapt the theme, story line, length and style of story to the developmental stage, particular interests and learning style of individual babies and children.

Young babies (0-11 months)

Use a bright sing-song voice to create two or three line songs, rhymes or stories around everyday routines, such as getting dressed, washing and so on. Try including the baby's name. Don't worry if the words make a nonsense rhyme, it is the sense of shared fun that is most important. Encourage older babies to imitate actions such as pointing to a door, or coat, or perhaps raising their arms up high in imitation of you for 'Pick me up please'.

Developmental Stage 1

Babies (8-20 months)

An exaggerated gasp or a gentle blow on a hand can be effective attention grabbers for babies at this development stage, as is varying your voice from a gentle whisper to a happy sing-song – be gentle, some babies are easily frightened by the unexpected. Create two or three simple action stories using favourite toys such as feeding, then washing teddy and then saying 'Night Night Ted!', as you talk through each stage of the story of Teddy's bedtime.

Developmental Stage 2

Young children (16-26 months)

Create a special 'My Day' story board for each child. Take photos of key parts of the child's day, such as arriving, playing, going outside, mealtimes, getting washed and so on. Use Velcro dots to fix the pictures to a board and build a simple story of the child's day. Be sure to give the child's story a clear and happy ending. Encourage children to tell their own stories of things that really happen to them or stories they make up.

Children (22-36 months)

Share a familiar object or photo of an object, and work together to create a simple story. Maybe use a digital camera to record the story or create scenes using play people, toy animals, cars and trains. Children will love a disaster with a happy ending, and heroes are important. Let the children take the lead in shaping the story and help them to create satisfying endings as they begin to understand that stories need a beginning, a middle and an end.

Older children (36-60+ months)

At this stage, children will really enjoy making story books themselves. They can use their own special interests, a favourite story or character, or an object such as an old key to get started. Record the story with the child's own drawings, Google images, photos taken by the child with a digital camera or perhaps cut from old magazines and brochures. There are lots of interesting websites with ideas and templates for making simple books.

Tales from other cultures

Sharing stories from around the world tells young children that you respect and value the views and cultures of other people living different lives with perhaps different traditions. It reinforces the fact that all over the world children have the same feelings, needs and fears and that people live in very different circumstances.

Young babies (0-11 months)

Ask parents to share their babies' favourite songs and their own best remembered stories of early childhood. Make tapes together of songs and rhymes in the baby's first language or dialect. Provide a range of interesting objects from a wide range of different cultures for young babies to explore. Listen to music from around the world and ensure that images around the setting, and in books and displays, represent different cultures.

Babies (8-20 months)

Look for simple board and picture books that include stories from around the world, but still remain focused on homes and everyday life. There are plenty of dual language board books and board books with multicultural images, which should be available from your local library service. Also look out for board books and simple picture books that have images representing children and families with dual heritage.

Developmental Stage 1

Developmental Stage 2

Tell simple stories focused on objects and pictures from other cultures and be sure that the everyday objects you provide in treasure baskets and other play represent a wide range of cultures. Keep storytelling sessions short and focused. Give the session a clear beginning signal, and a familiar and easily recognised end. Invite other adults from different backgrounds and cultures to visit to tell stories or bring objects and clothing to share with the children.

Simple picture books depicting tales from around the world provide children with knowledge and information about how other people live. Make this real with multi-sensory props, such as fabrics, containers, food and cooking utensils related to the story. Encourage older children to make links between their own experiences and those of the characters in the story. Involve parents and extended family members in sharing their own traditions.

Offer children at this developmental stage a wealth of stories and non-fiction books from across the globe, told or read from books to provide positive role models for all children and promoting understanding of diversity. Ask open ended questions to encourage children to think critically. Help children to see similarities in the stories with those from their own cultures. Continue to expand the range of props, characters and costumes for storytelling.

Developmental Stage 3

Developmental Stages 4 & 5

Developmental Stages 5 & 6

Story sacks and story boards

Story sacks are bags containing a carefully chosen picture book, props and other related materials as well as ideas for linked activities. First developed by Neil Griffiths, these are now widely used across the EYFS. You can create your own story sacks, buy them, or borrow from libraries or Children's Centres.

Young babies (0-11 months)

Create simple story sacks with a board book, one simple prop, and a couple of related action rhymes. Add a picture list of everyday objects suitable for a treasure basket and talk all this through with parents before inviting them to share the story sack at home with their baby. Talk together about encouraging gestures and turn taking. Invite parents to tell you about their baby's favourite board book or rhyme, so you can create a story sack unique to that baby.

Developmental Stage 1

Babies (8-20 months)

Babies will love to empty and refill the story sack. Find objects and books that are manageable for small fingers. Choose favourite picture books with plenty of opportunities for interaction, and use your imagination in adding small toys, puppets, soft toy animals etc.
Visit the National Literacy Trust website for more ideas or visit: www.storysack.com for lots of different story sacks to buy.

Developmental Stage 2

Young children (16-26 months)

Choose some favourite picture books that encourage language, such as 'Peepo' by Janet and Allan Ahlberg. Provide pairs of objects linked to the story in the story sack for lots of chances for matching games. Nursery rhyme tapes and CDs are perfect for parents to share with their child, maybe when travelling or at bedtime. Include ideas for other play related to the story, including outdoor and active play as well as games that include older siblings.

Children (22-36 months)

Story sacks are great for grabbing and maintaining the attention of children. You could add a puppet to tell a simple story, or for an element of anticipation, have a small number of simple props in a set of small boxes or a treasure box on your lap, revealing them one by one as the story develops. Choose extension activities carefully and they will appeal to children with a range of schemas. Read about schemas in 'Understanding Schemas in Young Children' by Stella Louis (Featherstone).

Older children (36-60+ months)

Story Boards are an ideal extension to the story sack idea for children at this stage.

Use large fabric shapes to represent characters and scenery, Velcro these to a board as you tell familiar

stories. Encourage children to get involved in the telling and placing the fabric pieces. You can also use the story board pieces to prompt children as they retell stories. Try creating story board pieces with children's drawings or Google images. For more story board ideas try 'The Little Book of Story Boards' (Featherstone).

Counting books

Counting books, with number songs, rhymes and stories are an important part of helping babies and young children learn about numbers, counting, matching and one-to-one correspondence – all essential foundations for problem solving, reasoning and numeracy across the EYFS and beyond.

Young babies (0-11 months)

Singing simple rhymes with number words are a great introduction for even the tiniest babies. Link words to actions, such as *'Round and round the garden like a Teddy Bear'*, or *'This Little Piggy'*. Looking at photo books and finding and talking about parts of the body, such as two eyes, two hands, one nose and so on are great first counting activities with books.

Developmental Stage 1

Babies (8-20 months)

Babies love stories with repetition and there are hundreds of counting books to choose from. Look for simple books with strong illustrations which concentrate on counting to five, preferably reinforcing the learning with counting songs and rhymes. Tell your own counting and number stories using groups of everyday objects, such as cups, spoons, shoes. Matching objects to pictures in a book is a great way to get started on learning one-to-one correspondence.

Developmental Stage 2

Young children (16-26 months)

Young children love active play and a strong rhythm, so picture books depicting favourite counting rhymes, such as *'Hickory Dickory Dock'*, or *'Five Elephants went out to play'* are always a hit. Board books with textured objects to count are a great idea and really help children as they get familiar with number words and move towards one-to-one correspondence. *'The Very Hungry Caterpillar'* is a classic, and comes in several formats.

Children (22-36 months)

As well as the more obvious counting books, look for books where counting is a central part of the storyline, such as *'Ten Little Monkeys Jumping on the Bed'*, a book with finger holes by Tina Freeman. Look for counting books from zero to ten and, for children confident in their counting skills and understanding of number, explore counting books that count down from ten to zero. Make birthday books with candles to count.

Older children (36-60+ months)

The story of Noah's Ark is an ideal starting point for counting in twos. Use small world animals to help children create and count in twos. Try making your own number stories using a bag of tiny objects as a prop. Take turns to add phrases with numbers to a standard sentence, such as 'The jolly pirate sailed the seven seas and in his treasure box he found … ten diamonds, a hundred gems', and so on. Use ICT with a paint program to create pages for a counting book.

Developmental Stage 3

Developmental Stages 4 & 5

Developmental Stages 5 & 6

Objects and pictures

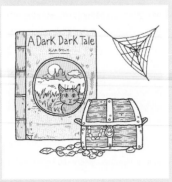

Everyday or unusual objects, pictures, photos or fact books all make excellent starting points for creating stories for and with the children. Such bespoke story making allows you to create tales that are well suited to individual interests and schemas of the children in the group.

Use everyday objects and a singing style to create simple three or four line 'mini stories', with opportunities for imitating simple gestures and actions. Using the baby's own favourite soft toy is a great way of capturing attention. Sit with the baby so they are sitting sideways on to you, so you can see their expression and they can easily give you eye contact. Give the baby the object to hold and explore as you tell the story.

Choose unusual and interesting objects to use with older babies. Make sure they are all safe for the babies to handle and mouth. Include objects which are smaller representations of larger objects, such as toy cars and animals. Large photos of single objects or people will also make good starting points. Keep story lines simple, and make the stories very short with big actions to copy. See 'This Little Puffin' by Elizabeth Matterson and other nursery rhyme collections for ideas.

Young children (16-26 months)

At this stage, children are fascinated by miniatures, such as play people, small animals and vehicles. Use this interest to spark the idea for a simple story. Give each child a miniature to hold or place down as you read or tell a story. Try starting with a simple commentary as young children play with a car or train set. Use their play as a starting point and then extend the scenes with a simple story line. Crashes and a happy ending are always popular!

Children (22-36 months)

Use exciting and unusual objects, such as tins or boxes, jewellery, items of clothing and foodstuffs as well as natural objects, and build short stories around them. Keep things simple. Plan the story line but be flexible and change your plans to include the children's own ideas. Make a note of the key points of the story as children love repetition and they are sure to want this special story, created just for them, over and over again.

Older children (36-60+ months)

Unusual images, photos of faraway places and children from other countries are all great starting places for story making. Show the children exciting objects, with a wide range of textures, smells, patterns and shapes.

Encourage the children to get involved in the story making by modelling your story on a familiar book with a strong text, such as 'A Dark Dark Tale' by Ruth Brown or following the format of a traditional tale, such as 'The Billy Goats Gruff'.

Developmental Stage 3

Developmental Stages 4 & 5

Developmental Stages 5 & 6

Pop-up and lift the flap books

Books that encourage babies and young children to physically explore the pages are great for grabbing and keeping attention. They also encourage older babies and children to share surprise and enjoyment with you. Later in the EYFS, books with flaps and pop-up sections can illustrate difficult concepts with ease.

Young babies (0-11 months)

Books with ribbons to grab or textures to explore are perfect at this stage, as well as soft fabric books to squeeze. Try black and white books to grab visual attention, but look for books with plenty of opportunities for holding, squeezing, pressing and grasping too. Try simple board books that have a textured last page – these are a great tactile reward. 'Lift the flap' books with an animal on each page are great for playing with sounds together.

Babies (8-20 months)

Try simple board books with mirrors on each page as a great way of playing peek-a-boo and naming parts of the face with older babies. Look for books with holes to poke – good for isolating index fingers and great for fun interactive play and tickle finger games. First 'lift the flap' books need to be sturdy, well illustrated, clear and focused on simple everyday routines familiar to babies and very young children, such as bath time and meal time.

Young children (16-26 months)

At this stage, it is crucial to get the balance right. Too much to fiddle with can distract such young children from the page. Look for books that have the 'lift the flap' detail, on the final page, rather than every page. Eric Hill's lovable little dog Spot is a great favourite for this age. Make your own 'lift the flap' book with photos, or pictures cut from magazines. Instructions for making your own books with children are widely available on the Internet.

Developmental Stage 3

Children (22-36 months)

At this stage, help small groups of young children to take turns to lift the flap. It often helps to give each child a small soft toy to hold or hug as they listen to the story and wait for their turn to lift the flap. Look for books with detailed illustrations for lots of searching, and books such as 'Pumpkin Soup' by Helen Cooper, which has opportunities for interaction on every page. Simple, durable pop-up books will become firm favourites for many children.

Developmental Stages 4 & 5

Older children (36-60+ months)

There are plenty of fact books with pop- up and lift the flap opportunities that will help children to sustain their attention on new information and ideas. Also look for story books with pop-up scenery to depict key scenes in longer stories. These offer lots of opportunities for talking and listening and prompting with open questions. Remember to encourage older children to share simpler interactive board books with babies and young children.

Developmental Stages 5 & 6

Family tales

Making your own simple books for storytelling is a great way of encouraging children to talk about their own families, their lives and experiences and to make connections between their worlds and those of others. This is also a very good way of involving parents in a key person activity.

Ask parents to help you take five or six simple, clear digital photos of key people in the baby's life. Print and laminate these. (Be sure to round the corners of the laminated cards and check that they are safe for small fingers.) Collect everyday objects that are familiar to the baby, such as their teddy or other soft toys, cup, spoon, car, and so on. Create a treasure basket of objects and pictures for exploring and sharing, and make the photos into books.

Create simple 'About me' books using digital photos, bits of fabric and small objects to explore, each tied with ribbon to the pages – a plastic spoon for the meal time page, a glove for going out, a bit of towel for the washing page. Personalise each book with a handprint. Include lots of different textures to explore, and add pictures of favourite toys from catalogues and magazines. Or make an 'About me' story board with objects and just one photo.

Developmental Stage 1

Developmental Stage 2

Young children (16-26 months)

Use digital photos to create a simple slide show that even very young children can operate by pressing a key or the space bar on a keyboard. Focus the story on everyday routines and use simple repetitive key phrases. Collect a basket of objects for parts of the child's day: a toothbrush, comb, flannel, spoon, hat, socks, book, baby blanket. Sing 'Here we go round the Mulberry Bush' with actions such as 'this is the way name pulls on a hat' and so on.

Children (22-36 months)

At this stage, children love to look at pictures of themselves when they were babies. Ask parents for photos and make a book showing each child growing up. Make simple 'lift the flap' books or concertina style fold out books or give each page a unique shape or border. This will tell the child how much their life story and contribution is valued. Invite parents and grandparents to join in making the book by providing photos and objects to share.

Older children (36-60+ months)

Encourage older children to use a simple digital camera to create their own pictures for an 'About me' tale, or a 'Three things about me that are special' book encouraging

children to talk about their strengths, interests and talents and to create a simple book to share that illustrates these three special things. Read story books that reflect the different ways families are made up. Every child should feel their family is valued and that all families are different.

Developmental Stage 3

Developmental Stages 4 & 5

Developmental Stages 5 & 6

Tall tales and nonsense

Stories with strange and wonderful text and illustrations are hugely important in creating a sense of fun and magic. Nonsense rhymes and silly stories inspire creativity and enthuse children with all aspects of story making and story telling. They also offer lots of opportunity for playing with sounds and words.

Young babies (0-11 months)

First play with words, simply making silly noises and imitating vocalisations are the forerunners of first nonsense rhymes. Try taking a familiar babble sound and simply repeating it at different speeds, using a whisper, a sing-song or a croaky voice. Play with sounds and offer babies lots of chances to copy the sounds and create sounds for you to copy. This sort of reciprocal, turn-taking vocal play is critical to babies' early language development.

Developmental Stage 1

Babies (8-20 months)

Babies love nursery and nonsense rhymes. Try creating your own magical creatures, such as Nelly the Jelly, and play with the words, offering blobs of jelly to squeeze as you sing, rhyme and play together. It is never too soon to introduce children to poetry. For a very first poem board book, try 'Here's A Little Poem' by Jane Yolen, or try the engaging rhyming story 'Polar Bear Polar Bear, What do you See?' by Eric Carle.

Developmental Stage 2

Young children (16-26 months)

Listening to nonsense stories and poems is not just fun but is reassuring, builds listening skills and gives a great sense of shared purpose or attention. Very young children will enjoy Michael Rosen's 'Poems for the Very Young'. Other first poetry books include 'The Hairy Hamster and Other Poems About Pets' by Tony Bradman, or 'The Happy Hedgehog Band' by Martin Waddell, which both have great text and magical illustrations.

Children (22-36 months)

Try Edward Lear for nonsense rhymes and pictures, as well as poems such as 'The Daddy Long Legs and the Fly' – find these at www.nonsenselit.org/Lear. Dr Seuss and Ogden Nash wrote great collections of silliness. Other favourites at this stage are picture books with all the pages divided horizontally into three parts that can be turned independently of each other to create endless combinations of silly pictures and nonsense, or you could make your own.

Older children (36-60+ months)

Create your own lists of rhyming nonsense. Start with a standard phrase, such as 'The monkey went to the shops and bought an apple' encourage the children to make up words that rhyme with apple, and call out 'The monkey went to the shops and bought an apple, papple, napple, wapple' and so on. Don't worry if they don't make sense. Just keep the rhythm going, and use a slow drum beat to keep up the pace. Record your rhymes for listening later.

Objects of wonder

Providing a rich collection of objects to explore and wonder at, to enjoy for their feel, smell and shape rather than to understand their function enables children to explore the world beyond the everyday. The objects can then be used to spark children's own commentary and storytelling.

Young babies (0-11 months)

When considering objects of wonder to provide for babies at this age they must be safe, easy to handle and enticing for multi-sensory exploration. Look for objects with unusual textures and shapes in the everyday as well as the natural world. Sing a simple commentary for the baby, describing their actions, such as 'squish, squeeze', or 'shake, shake, shake'. Use mobiles and other visually interesting objects to encourage looking.

Developmental Stage 1

Babies (8-20 months)

The natural world provides endless objects of wonder for babies at this stage. Look for objects that they can explore in a very active way, and create rhymes and stories to reinforce their discoveries. Try kicking or stamping in dry leaves, splashing through puddles and so on, and then pretend to be a dinosaur stomping along. Encourage the babies to imitate your actions as well as taking the time to imitate theirs.

Developmental Stage 2

Young children (16-26 months)

Make objects of wonder extra special by presenting them inside a bag or special box, or perhaps on a special cushion. Ensure objects are easy to handle, familiar to the child and offer plenty of 'feedback' when explored, such as a big bunch of keys, a torch or maybe a wind up toy. Mechanical objects and dressing up clothes and jewellery are ideal objects of wonder to spark a simple storytelling session with children at this stage.

Children (22-36 months)

Invite the children to examine objects with plastic magnifying glasses, or through mirrors and lenses. Watching objects grow also produces a great sense of wonder. Link these with stories about growing, such as 'Titch' by Pat Hutchins, or 'The Very Hungry Caterpillar'. Using multi-sensory story props will enable children with a wide range of learning styles to become more involved and absorbed in the storytelling.

Older children (36-60+ months)

Children can now examine objects in much greater depth. Provide a wide range of really unusual objects for children to wonder at and to inspire their fantasy worlds. Circle time is a great time to look at a curious object or picture and to create a storyline together. Try using a story board to record the story created during these sessions. Encourage children to find their own objects of wonder and suggest their own stories about them.

Developmental Stage 3

Developmental Stages 4 & 5

Developmental Stages 5 & 6

Rhyming text

Babies and children love rhyme. The rhythm of the text and the way the words bounce off the tongue are a great way to hold attention. The rhythm provides a focus and builds a sense of anticipation across the story. Understanding and enjoying rhythm and rhyme are essential in learning to read.

Young babies (0-11 months)

Choose first rhymes with a strong rhythm and repetition, such as '*Round and Round the Garden Like a Teddy Bear*' or '*This Little Pig went to market*'. Reinforce the rhythm with actions, as in knee jigging rhymes such as '*Ride a Cock Horse*' and '*Giddy up and Away we Go*' all from '*The Mother Goose Nursery Rhyme Collection*' by Daniel San Souci.

Developmental Stage 1

Babies (8-20 months)

At this stage, expand the repertoire of rhymes, with rhymes from around the world. Check out the collection at www.mamalisa.com or try Floella Benjamin's collection '*Skip Across the Ocean*'. For picture books with a great rhyming text, visit the Book Trust recommended titles for under fives – www.booktrust.org.uk has a searchable database of children's books, including rhyming books, or you could try *Amazon* for rhyming story books.

Developmental Stage 2

Young children (16-26 months)

Choose simple stories around everyday routines, such as *'Is it Bedtime Wibbly Pig?'* by Mick Inkpen. Also try rhymes that encourage children to imitate boisterous big actions and make lots of noise, such as *'We're going on a Bear Hunt'* by Michael Rosen, *'Monkey See, Monkey Do'* by Allan Ahlberg, or *'Jen the Hen'*, *'Tog the Dog'*, *'Pat the Cat'*, *'Mig the Pig'*, a series of simple rhyming tales by Colin and Jacqui Hawkins.

Children (22-36 months)

Explore rhyming verse as well as rhyming stories. Be sure to choose books with a strong rhyming text but that also have a great opening, a strong story line and a satisfying ending. Try *'Where's My Teddy?'* by Jez Alborough, *'Llama, Llama, Red Pajama'* by Anne Dewdney or *'The Gruffalo'* and *'Gruffalo's Child'* by Julia Donaldson. At this stage also try simple rhymes from nursery rhyme anthologies as well as dipping into first poems.

Older children (36-60+ months)

Anushka Ravishankar's picture books with strong stories and exciting rhyming text introduce older children to another world. Try *'Catch That Crocodile'*. Or perhaps try creating strings of rhyming words, or adapting the text of favourite rhyming story books, such as *'Hairy Maclary'* by Lynley Dodd, or *'Pass the Jam Jim'* by Kaye Umanski. Scan children's own illustrations of these into a computer and create your own digital story books.

Developmental Stage 3

Developmental Stages 4 & 5

Developmental Stages 5 & 6

Little stories, big actions

All babies and children love action songs and stories, and they are perfect for wrigglers and kinesthetic learners across the EYFS stages. Using movement encourages memory and a sense of rhythm, essential for learning to communicate, and eventually in learning to read.

Young babies (0-11 months)

Use baby signing and natural gesture, pointing and clapping to get babies involved in simple stories. Imitating actions and sounds is a critical pre-verbal skill for children, and the use of signs and gestures help develop situational and first understanding of familiar words and phrases. Babies generally love gentle tumble play, swinging carefully and safely from side to side and up and down.

Developmental Stage 1

Babies (8-20 months)

'All fall down' is a great phrase and action in songs and stories for older babies and very young children. At this stage, rocking back and forth and side to side are all actions that can be incorporated into simple stories, as well as bouncing and jigging. To help children maintain their attention on the story or picture book, keep to just a few actions linked very clearly with key phrases in the story.

Developmental Stage 2

Young children (16-26 months)

About now, children love to hold a soft toy during story time and can create their own simple pretend play actions to mimic a story line. This is a great way of reinforcing the story and helping children to remain focused. For more fun with storytelling use a very familiar story and with an exaggerated gasp and pause, substitute actions for words. This really builds anticipation and keeps children focussed on the text or story line.

Children (22-36 months)

Try stories that allow children to imitate your actions or create their own to express what they understand by the story. Try some scary stories such as '*Not Now Bernard*' by David McKee, as these allow children to blend humour with fear and take the sting out of the tale. '*Follow My Leader*' by Emma Chichester Clark is a great movement story, with a steady beat, and '*It's the Bear*' and the others in the series by Jez Alborough are made for movement.

Older children (36-60+ months)

At this stage children might like to work together with actions, such as in '*The Enormous Turnip*' by Jan Lewis, or '*Room on the Broom*' by Julia Donaldson. This is a great time to plan for co-operative play, negotiating and turn taking. Children will also enjoy changing the location of story time, perhaps sharing stories outside, or in the home corner, or even under a blanket by torch light. Try and link the venue and props to the focus of the story.

Stories with puppets

Throughout the EYFS, the emphasis is on learning through play, story, rhymes and music. Get great puppets from:
www.puppetsforeducation.co.uk
www.puppetsbypost.com
www.chelltune.co.uk (for flat glove puppets), _www. cambridgeeducationaltoys. co.uk_ (for hiding puppets linked to familiar stories).

Young babies (0-11 months)

Even tiny babies enjoy finger play and a single finger puppet is a great way to engage babies' attention, develop visual skills, encourage reaching and reinforce finger rhyme and tickle games. Allow plenty of time for each baby to explore the puppet. _www.chelltune.co.uk_ also have an interesting range of resources to support baby signing and early communication.

Developmental Stage 1

Babies (8-20 months)

At this stage, babies are learning to copy actions, so use natural gestures and clap hands. Simple puppets made from socks, mittens or gloves are a great way to build these skills, alongside very simple picture and board books, as well as familiar nursery rhymes. It is a great idea to give the baby a puppet that matches yours, to encourage interaction, silly or sensible discussions, turn taking and imitation.

Developmental Stage 2

Young children (16-26 months)

'Hiding puppets' are great for children at this stage in the EYFS. They are usually a main puppet that opens up to reveal more finger puppets, such as an owl mummy who opens her wings to reveal owl baby finger puppets, ideal for the popular picture book 'Owl Babies' by Martin Waddell. Make other puppets special by letting them peek around a story book. For hiding puppets visit: www.cambridgeducationaltoys.co.uk or your local toy library.

Children (22-36 months)

At this stage, children will enjoy all types of puppets used as props to support stories told and read from picture books. Puppets are available commercially in sets with some of the most popular early years picture books. Simple sock and glove puppets are easy to make and a great project for older children. At this stage, some children may find large puppets confusing and potentially alarming, so allow plenty of time for 'getting to know you' activities.

Older children (36-60+ months)

Older children will enjoy making their own puppets, perhaps wooden spoon puppets, finger puppets, glove or sock puppets. Encourage them to retell favourite stories with their puppets, focusing on traditional tales and familiar themes such as 'People who help us'. Puppets are a great resource to support story time for children for whom English is an additional language, and access to puppets for free play and story telling should be a part of every room.

Developmental Stage 3

Developmental Stages 4 & 5

Developmental Stages 5 & 6

If you find this book useful
you might also like to look at ...

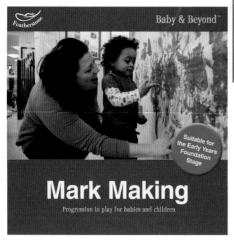

All available from www.bloomsbury.com